THE JOYS OF
ENGRISH

THE JOYS OF ENGRISH

Steven Caires

Jeremy P. Tarcher/Penguin · a member of Penguin Group (USA) Inc. · New York

JEREMY P. TARCHER/PENGUIN
Published by the Penguin Group

Penguin Group (USA) Inc., 375 Hudson Street, New York, New York 10014, USA · Penguin Group (Canada), 90 Eglinton Avenue East, Suite 700, Toronto, Ontario M4P 2Y3, Canada (a division of Pearson Penguin Canada Inc.) · Penguin Books Ltd, 80 Strand, London WC2R 0RL, England · Penguin Ireland, 25 St Stephen's Green, Dublin 2, Ireland (a division of Penguin Books Ltd) · Penguin Group (Australia), 250 Camberwell Road, Camberwell, Victoria 3124, Australia (a division of Pearson Australia Group Pty Ltd) · Penguin Books India Pvt Ltd, 11 Community Centre, Panchsheel Park, New Delhi–110 017, India · Penguin Group (NZ), Cnr Airborne and Rosedale Roads, Albany, Auckland 1310, New Zealand (a division of Pearson New Zealand Ltd) · Penguin Books (South Africa) (Pty) Ltd, 24 Sturdee Avenue, Rosebank, Johannesburg 2196, South Africa

Penguin Books Ltd, Registered Offices: 80 Strand, London WC2R 0RL, England

Most Tarcher/Penguin books are available at special quantity discounts for bulk purchase for sales promotions, premiums, fund-raising, and educational needs. Special books or book excerpts also can be created to fit specific needs. For details, write Penguin Group (USA) Inc. Special Markets, 375 Hudson Street, New York, NY 10014.

Library of Congress Cataloging-in-Publication Data

Caires, Steven.
The joys of Engrish / Steven Caires.
p.   cm.
ISBN 1-58542-452-8
1. English language—Japan—Humor.   2. English language—Japan—Pictorial works.
3. English language—Japan—Errors of usage—Humor.   I. Title: Joys of Engrish.   II. Title.
PN6231.E74C35   2005   2005048523
428'.00952—dc22

Printed in China
1 3 5 7 9 10 8 6 4 2

This book is printed on acid-free paper. ∞

Book design by Stephanie Huntwork

Introduction

Engrish: More than a word, it's a cultural phenomenon. And it has begun attracting attention across the English-speaking world. Surprising English phrases, ranging from the quaint to the profane, have long appeared in Japanese advertising and product design. They are apparently there only to make products and services look cool to the Japanese public, but observe what happens when we dig a little deeper: Somehow, oddball truths seem to emerge. Irony, existentialism, and dark humor appear where only fun-loving phraseology had been intended.

We may never entirely understand the processes at hand, but it cannot be denied that Engrish can yield kernels of wisdom, beauty and profundity. Indeed, there exist moments of mysterious poetic wit and subtle nuance that transcend the art form. Witness the postcard of a squirrel discussing "delicious walnut:"

"I am always full of appetite. Then, it is fine." These are the squirrel's words.

Indeed it is fine. What can be finer to the innocent squirrel than being full of walnuts? Is this not a metaphor for the human condition? Once we fulfill our core needs in life as the squirrel has, should we not all be fine? But the squirrel is always full of appetite. Touché.

Now consider a t-shirt featuring two bananas exchanging pleasantries: "All yellow? Or flecked with brown man!?" Notice how the all-yellow banana has been daringly peeled, yet the banana flecked with brown remains sealed within his skin. Which one are you?

Take yet another popular shirt: "Crap. What Kind of World Is This? It's Kind of Crap!" Is the existential message here intentional or unintentional? Does it matter?

It is surely no coincidence that the message boards at Engrish.com have attracted an intellectual crowd of native English speakers from around the globe. The most popular feature of the boards is the "Speak in Engrish" forum, where thousands of board members compose their own versions of Engrish based on the hundreds of samples found on the main site. Each new "Engrish of the Day" image at Engrish.com adds to the lexicon of the "Engrish" language and is celebrated through its adoption by the board members. The fact that the message boards have retained a friendly, yet intellectually stimulating, atmosphere is a testament to the power of Engrish.

For those new to Engrish, I am confident you will come to share my own belief that there is something here that can be appreciated on many levels and on multiple occasions.

Please make sure to enjoy your pleasant with vigor!

Steven Caires
creator of Engrish.com

THE JOYS OF
ENGRISH

My friend is dead
on Monday.
It was a
sunny day.
I feel sick
I feel so blue.
I pray to Jesus.

I HATE MY LIFE I HATE MY FRIENDS
I HATE THE SUN I HATE THIS WORLD
I HATE YOUR RELIGION
I DON'T BELIEVE IN JESUS CHRIST
AND ANY GODS
I HAVE NINE HEADS
BUT THEY'RE NOT THINKIN' VERY FAST

run at full speed with
the aim of the freedom
it is the thing of the necessity to look for freedom for the human being

Reserch

THE CREATION OF NEW INFORMATION
IN THE INFINITY

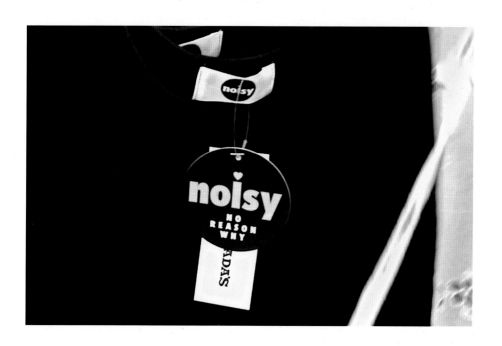

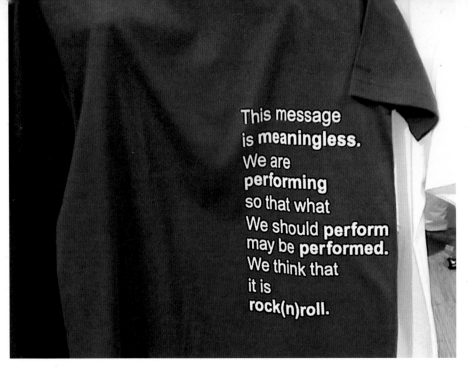

This message
is **meaningless.**
We are
performing
so that what
We should **perform**
may be **performed.**
We think that
it is
rock(n)roll.

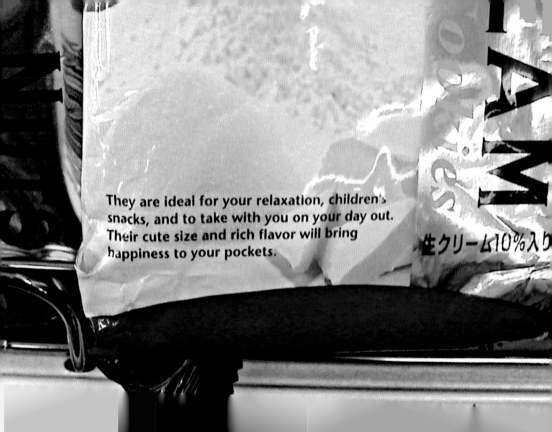

They are ideal for your relaxation, children's snacks, and to take with you on your day out. Their cute size and rich flavor will bring happiness to your pockets.

生クリーム10%入り

HOXY will always offer
you a rich and comfortable
life with paper.

Pied O Beautyful

Glory be to God for dappled things-
For skies of couple-color as a brinded cow;

14

McKINLEY

We made this specially for you. Man can't
exist without air and water and this bag.
We must trust to divine providence.

DESPERATION
ALL HOPE AND DREAMS GOING NO WHERE
SO WE PRAY FOR A NEW TOMORROW

TO WASH OUR SORROWS AWAY

There's a begger,
Feels like harf a man he fought the war, now he fight the pain
He was a hero in a foreign land. Now he's flat broke and stranded in the rain
But. his dignity runs deeper than the ocean

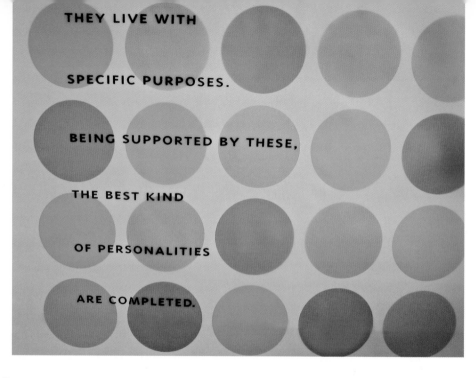

THEY LIVE WITH

SPECIFIC PURPOSES.

BEING SUPPORTED BY THESE,

THE BEST KIND

OF PERSONALITIES

ARE COMPLETED.

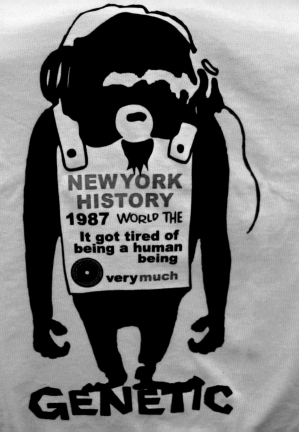

CONSISTENCY PAINTER

Paint with which the dangerous substance was mixed...

21

Artless Children

**We were so absorbed in the games
that we had forgotten all about the time.**

WONDER LASTS BUT

1977

Nine Days

FIGHT
PEACEFUL

Swarms
of winter gnats
are still around

yand the gentle
wartling and
chattering

25

27

You're Very The Highest.

Prisoner of

You're Very The Highest society

society

Dryness Of The Heart

Only The Strong Survives

It's Our Brand in the attic

simple

**I fall in love with you.
You are my favorite food.**

¥500.000BANK

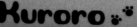

Kuroro

He is a black cat and a name is KURORO. Since he is lonely, he wants a friend.

2F

1週間無利息キャッシング

NO LOAN

SHREWD

A ruler dies three times.
It is stimulative.

•pastor's belief•

Confession

(for the best) teacher.

Experience is a good

preach

●DESPAIR GIVES COURAGE TO A COWARD●

DEEDS, NOT WORDS.

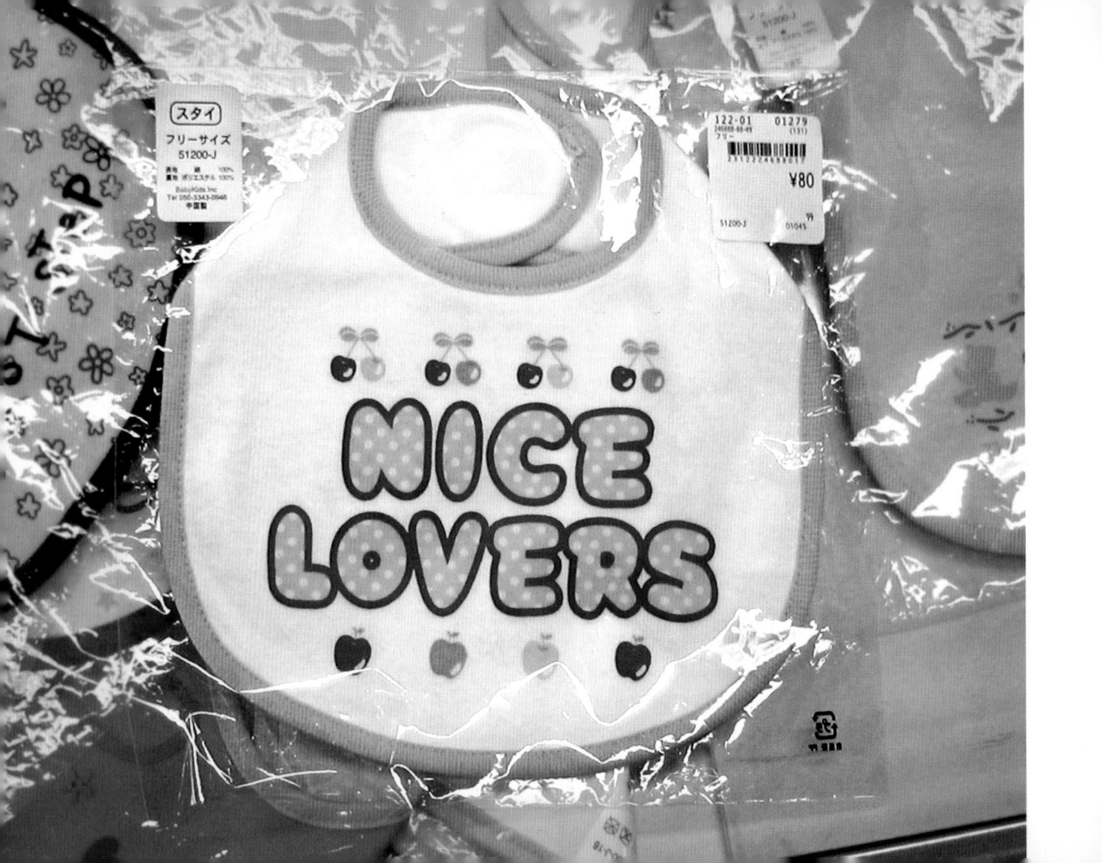
スタイ
フリーサイズ
51200-J
122-01 01279
¥80
NICE
LOVERS

39

40

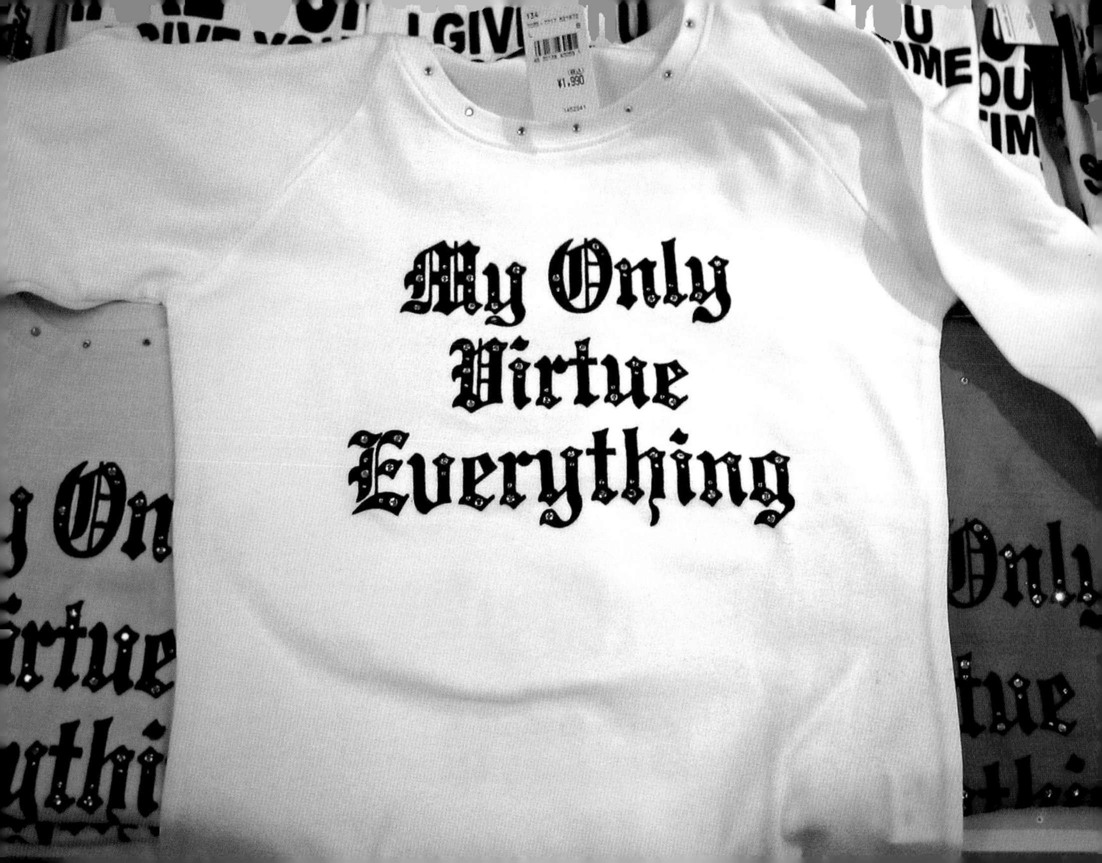
My Only
Virtue
Everything

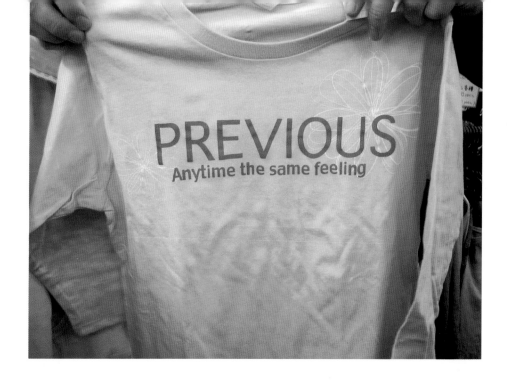

45

tea cup puppy

he is a very small puppy,
and he likes feeling
relieved in a tea cup.

POWER GiRL

You fond a treasure at last.
I have only a faint memory of that affair.
The scene still comes to mind now and then.
I have a vividly remember
seeing you here.

Bravo!

We think that it will always be with smile.
Then, a pleasant thing comes.

CUBIC ANIMALS
They are very pleasant friends.

Elephanto with sweet flower

All around us,
our own world of wonder!
Can't you see how chic we are?

GET OVER THE WALL

Never give up because we're dreamer.

52

COFFEE

Cafe

Hamburger   24h   Hot dog

THE MEETING
OF SUPPLY
AND DEMAND

CLOVER 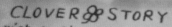 STORY
I wish to sing a duet with
transparent time.

You'll have mind to
forgive everything.

If you become angry
or nervous, hold communion
with nature.

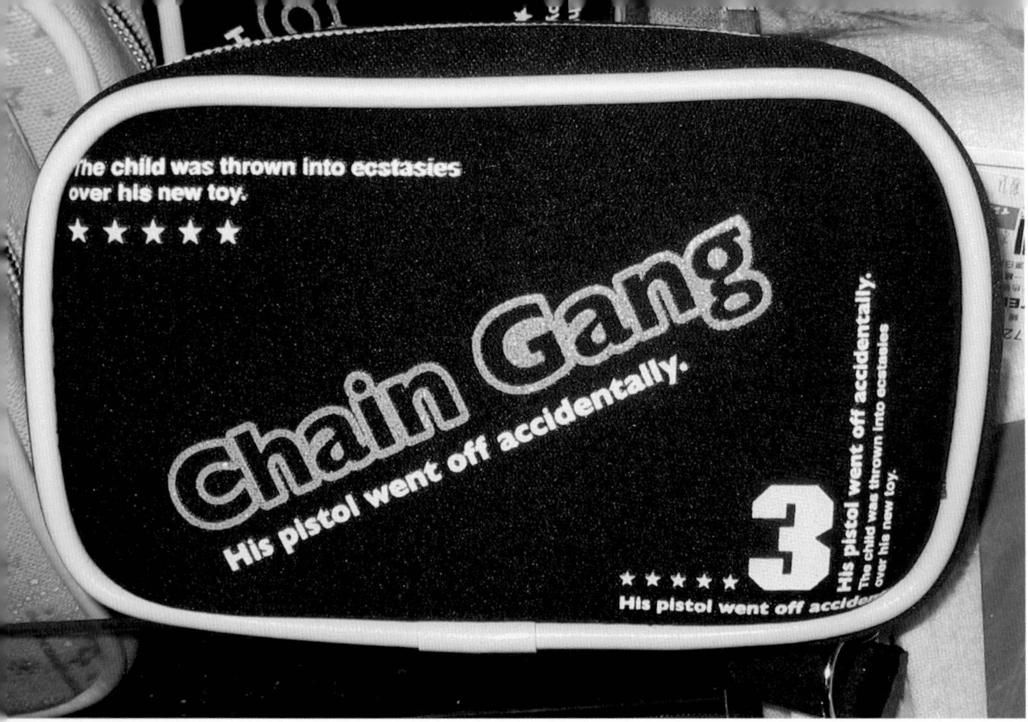

60

LILY BELL

It is living happily together wholly.
But it is also disagreeable to
become lonely although he
wants to come apart occasionally.

Did you have a good time yesterday?

I am painting for pleasure.

LIVE A HAPPY LIFE

Love cherry

Pleasant things…
I really love them!

I'm in a very fine mood. All are new. Anticipation of a wonderful encounter!!

198202

Hopes are at my side.

My dream that has begun to move. → → →

College

NOTEBOOK

*This is the most comfortable notebook
you have ever run into.*

30SHEETS

TITLE

POCKET
WETTY

● ポケット ウエッティー ●

OPEN ←

m glad to know
you're fine.

That is about all I want to tell you this time.

化粧室は後方へ
For Restrooms,
Go back toward your behind.

14   ↑   13

full of dreams and
full of hopes
my everyday is
american style
and very
Funnyday

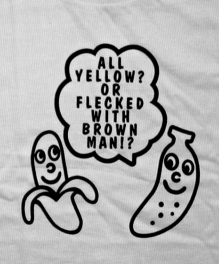

DANGER

BIOHAZARD

IT SUPPOSED TO HELP
ALL THE PEOPLE
IT SUPPOSED
TO MAKE THEM HAPPY
BUT WE GOT
TO RECOGNIZE IT DANGER

I wonder why coffee tastes so good when your'e naked with your family.

73

インターホン

Interphone

ご用のお客様は、インターホンで
係員におたずね下さい。

When you have something to do
please call the operation staff
by interphone.

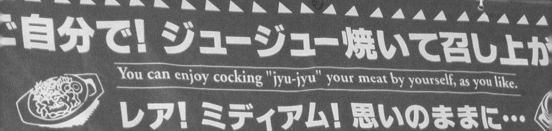

ご自分で! ジュージュー焼いて召し上が

You can enjoy cocking "jyu-jyu" your meat by yourself, as you like.

レア! ミディアム! 思いのままに…

ジュージュー焼いて召し

DY-151   ✦ MATSUNO HOBBY

快適生活雑貨

TOILET BRUSH

We'll advise you about your 'stickiness' about your daily life.
To the people enjoying their life…

品質表示	
材質	(毛部) ポリプロピレン
	(柄) ポリプロピレン
耐熱温度	60℃

MATSUNO INDUSTRY CO.,LTD.
2-3-67 URIWARIMINAMI, HIRANO-KU, OSAKA

4 978929 441517

MADE IN CHINA

袋:PP   ラベル

HAPPY DRUG

ハッピードラッグ 十和田店

くすり・化粧品・日用品

Hello!

Woody!

Do you want join in vehement athletics?

When anyone is living, there are various happening

A happy thing. A sad thing. A hard day comes in the tim

But, anyone is living very har

LOOK, BLOOD.

献血友だちに
なってください。

宝くじ号

LET'S BEGIN
TO LOVE MYSELF
OVER AGAIN

MONKEY BROTHERS

HELP

MONKEY BROTHERS

© 1999 by R.U.P

This pleasant group is always
good company, and they
have superb fashion sense.

オナラの時の後方確認。
たばこの時は忘れてた。

Before passing gas
I look behind me.
But I don't bother
when I'm smoking.

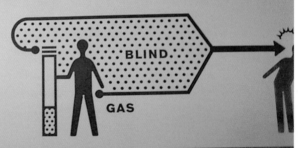

BLIND

GAS

FORWARD ←

TOBACCO

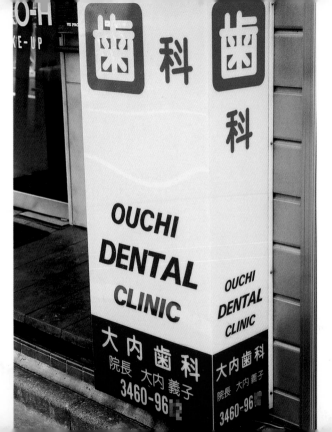

歯 科 歯
科

OUCHI

DENTAL

CLINIC

OUCHI
DENTAL
CLINIC

大内歯科
院長 大内 義子
3460-96

大内歯科
院長 大内 義子
3460-96

95

TITTY BOO
TOWER

7F TITTYBOO PARTY ROOM
6F TITTYBOO PARTY ROOM
5F TITTYBOO PARTY ROOM
4F TITTYBOO PARTY ROOM
3F TITTYBOO PARTY ROOM
2F TITTYBOO WEDDING DRESS
1F TITTYBOO RECEPTION ROOM
B1 TITTYBOO MACHINE ROOM
B2 TITTYBOO PARTY ROOM

TEL 03-5464-19

株式会社ティティーブーカンパニー
渋谷区渋谷3-1-7

Delicious
Walnut

I am always full of
appetite. Then, it is fine.

使用後は必ずこの釦を
押して下さい。

YOU LADY WILL PUSH
THIS BUTTON BEFORE
LEAVING.

Acknowledgments

The author would like to thank the following people for their contributions to Engrish.com, and for helping make this book possible:

Michael Degelbeck, John Russell, Fahruz, Mark Schreiber, Roger Lerud, Beth Hoover, Eric C. Smith, Cindy Carl, Taylor Metcalf, Wilson Rothman, Elena Nazvanova, Joe Grand, Greg Medlock, Brenda Johnson, Mark Hemmings, Shannon Poe-Kennedy and Justin Sheehy, Randy Schmidt, Scott Ehardt, Scott Murphy, Laura Conlon, Steven and Lisa Kohara, Richard Jew, Andrew Bowyer, Gareth Evans, Nick George, Carlos Sandoval and Royce Leong, Craig Thornton and Jess Jardine, Keith Kemerer, Jóhann Ingi Ólafsson, Lisa Bliss, Jason and Gloria Cancro, and Charles Rich.

About the Author

Steven Caires, founder of Engrish.com, started to collect Engrish in 1987, when he first went to Japan as a student. Over the course of ten years living in Tokyo, as both a student and "salaryman," he would frequently bring back Engrish candy, gum, and other small items to the United States as gifts for friends. In 1996, when the Internet was just starting to become mainstream, compiling Engrish on a website became a natural extension of his collection, and Engrish.com was born.